THE WORKING EXPERIENCE 1

BY JEANNE H. SMITH AND HARRY RINGEL

New Readers Press

Acknowledgments

The authors wish to express their sincere thanks to the following individuals and agencies without whose support *The Working Experience* would never have come to be:

Executive Directors Mike Blum and Rev. William Erat, of Nationalities Service Center and Lutheran Children and Family Service in Philadelphia, for providing the direction in their agencies which makes projects such as this one possible.

NSC Assistant Executive Director and Education Programs Coordinator Seki Howland, for her ongoing faith and input, especially as the role of LEA in this project evolved.

LCFS Community Services Manager Harriet Brener–Sam, for her support and interest in project direction.

Jim Biles and Barbara Buckley–Deni, instructors at Lutheran Children and Family Service, whose commitment and care were vital in preparing their students to be interviewed for this project.

JoAnn Weinberger, Executive Director of the Center for Literacy, Inc., who was always eager to listen to new ideas and willing to support our efforts.

Good Lad Inc. and Centro Pedro Claver, for extending the warmest of welcomes to our project.

The authors also extend their special thanks to all the ESL students who shared their working experiences and whose stories, which form the heart of *The Working Experience,* will now be shared with many others.

ISBN 0-88336-965-6

Copyright © 1991
New Readers Press
Publishing Division of Laubach Literacy International
Box 131, Syracuse, New York 13210

Printed in the United States of America

Project Editor: Paula Schlusberg
Manuscript Editor: Maria Collis
Publication Assistant: Jeanna H. Walsh
Designer: Kathleen T. Bates
Cover design: The W. D. Burdick Company

9 8 7 6 5 4

Table of Contents

Kirk Condyles, Impact Visuals

My Father's Store

I work in my father's store. The store is very small. It is very old, too. And it is in a very old neighborhood in the city. Asian people and black people shop in my father's store.

We have many customers because we make good sandwiches. We sell groceries, too. The customers can buy American food and Korean food. The children buy candy with their pennies, nickels, and dimes. They always come back. They like to stay and play in our store.

—**Soo Lim**
Korea

Comprehension

True or False

Write **T** or **F** for true or false.

_____ 1. Soo works in her uncle's store.

_____ 2. The store is big and new.

_____ 3. The store is outside the city.

_____ 4. Asian and black customers shop in this store.

_____ 5. Customers can buy things to eat in this store.

_____ 6. The store sells only American food.

Fill-in

Read the story again. Then write these words into the sentences.

black   old   many   small   good   play

1. My father's store is very _____ and very old.

2. It is in a very _____ neighborhood.

3. We have _____ customers in our store.

4. We make _____ sandwiches.

5. Asian people and _____ people shop in our store.

6. Children like to _____ in our store.

Language Skills

Vocabulary Review

Circle the correct word.

1. I go to the store to (shop, play) for food.
2. I live in an old (father, neighborhood).
3. I will make you a (sandwich, customer) for lunch.
4. Children like to eat (candy, nickels).
5. Many (sandwiches, customers) shop in that store.

Structure Practice

In English 's on the end of a word shows that something belongs to someone. Use the words below to fill in the blanks. Add 's to the first word. The first one is done for you.

1. Soo   father

_____Soo's_____ _____father_____ has a store.

2. customer   sandwich

The _____ _____ tastes good.

3. child   candy

This is the _____ _____ .

4. neighbor   groceries

The _____ _____ are on the table.

5. family   store

The _____ _____ is in an old neighborhood.

Word Families

Read and study:

Korea—Korean   Asia—Asian   America—American

Now circle the best word for each sentence.

1. Soo is from (Asia, Asian).
2. She speaks (Korea, Korean).
3. Now she lives in (American, America).
4. Many (Asia, Asian) people live in her neighborhood.
5. (Korea, Korean) is her native country.
6. She eats (America, American) food every day.

Number Work

Match the money word with the number for the amount.

penny   10¢
nickel   25¢
dime   5¢
quarter   1¢

Follow-up

Let's Talk about It

1. Where does Soo work?
2. Where is the store?
3. Who shops in this store?
4. Why do they have so many customers?
5. Why do children like this store?

What's Your Story?

Where do you work? Tell about the people at the place where you work.

2

The Boss

I won't work in a factory. Bosses in factories don't respect people or treat them equally. They sometimes scream and talk nasty. Bosses get better jobs and more money. Workers do the hard work and make less money.

—Josefina Rivera
Puerto Rico

Comprehension

True or False

Write **T** or **F** for true or false.

_____ 1. Josefina says workers get more money than bosses.

_____ 2. Josefina says bosses don't respect workers.

_____ 3. Josefina says bosses get better jobs.

_____ 4. Josefina won't work in a factory.

_____ 5. Josefina says workers sometimes scream.

_____ 6. Josefina says bosses do the hard work.

Complete the Sentence

Read the story again. Fill in the blanks with the appropriate words from the story. The first one is done for you.

1. I won't work in a ____factory____.

2. Bosses in factories don't _____ people.

3. Bosses don't treat people _____.

4. They sometimes _____ and talk nasty.

5. Bosses get better _____ and more money.

6. Workers do the hard work and make less _____.

Language Skills

Vocabulary Review

Circle the correct word.

1. Bosses sometimes (talk, work) nasty.
2. Factory workers do (hard, job) work.
3. Workers make less (respect, money).
4. Josefina won't work in a (boss, factory).
5. It is important to (work, respect) people.

Word Families

Draw a line from the activity to the person who does the activity. The first one is done for you.

Activity	Person
work	teacher
bake	worker
paint	baker
drive	painter
teach	driver

Structure Practice: Singular and Plural

Write the words for more than one.

1. one job   many _____

2. one worker   three _____

3. one teacher   five _____

4. one student   many _____

5. one car   two   _____

Follow-up

Let's Talk about It

For each question, tell Josefina's opinion, then your opinion.

1. Who gets better jobs?
2. Who does the hard work?
3. Who gets more money?
4. How do bosses treat workers?
5. Why won't Josefina work in a factory?

What's Your Story?

Do you have a good boss or a bad boss? Tell a story about your boss.

3

Marilyn Humphries, Impact Visuals

Day Off

On my day off, I look around my house for things to do. The first thing I do is clean the house. I also wash the clothes. Sometimes I sit down, drink a cup of coffee, and watch television. Later, I think about what I can cook for dinner.

On my day off, I sometimes go shopping with my sister. We look at everything in the stores. We eat a nice lunch in a restaurant.

—**Ligia Figueroa**
Colombia

Comprehension

True or False

The sentences below are about Ligia's day off. Write **T** or **F** for true or false.

_____ 1. Ligia cleans her house.

_____ 2. Ligia washes the clothes.

_____ 3. Sometimes, Ligia drinks a cup of tea.

_____ 4. Ligia goes shopping with her mother.

_____ 5. Ligia eats lunch in a restaurant.

_____ 6. Ligia goes to the movies.

Complete the Sentence

Read the story again. Fill in the blanks with the appropriate words from the story.

1. On my _____ off, I look around my house.

2. The first thing I do is _____ the house.

3. I _____ the clothes.

4. Sometimes, I _____ down, drink a cup of

   _____, and watch television.

5. Later, I think about what I can _____ for dinner.

6. On my day off, I sometimes go _____ with my sister.

7. We look at everything in the _____.

8. We eat a nice _____ in a restaurant.

Language Skills

Vocabulary Review

Circle the correct word.

1. I (drink, look) around the store for things to buy.
2. I (clean, think) the bedroom.
3. I (drink, wash) the dishes.
4. I (drink, look) a cup of tea and (think, watch) television.
5. We (eat, look) at people on the street.

Capital Letters: Beginning Sentences

Capital letters begin sentences. The sentences below are from the story.
Read each sentence. Write the beginning capital letter. The first one
is done for you.

1. __O__n my day off, I look around my house for things to do.

2. _____he first thing I do is clean the house.

3. _____ometimes, I sit down, drink a cup of coffee, and watch television.

4. _____e look at everything in the stores.

5. _____e eat a nice lunch in a restaurant.

Structure Practice

Match the words that go together. The first one is done for you.

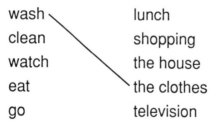

wash   lunch
clean   shopping
watch   the house
eat   the clothes
go   television

Follow-up

Let's Talk about It

1. What is the first thing Ligia does on her day off?
2. What does Ligia wash?
3. What does Ligia watch on television?
4. Who does Ligia go shopping with?
5. Where do they eat?
6. Do you think Ligia has fun on her day off? Why?

What's Your Story?

What do you do on your day off?

THE BETTMANN ARCHIVE

My First Job

My name is Alberta. I work in a clothing factory. I use a special sewing machine. It makes stitches to finish hems and seams. I sew linings into clothes with this machine.

I work with about 40 or 50 other workers. We all do the same job. We all get along with one another. I think this is a good job.

—Alberta Henderson
Lithuania

Comprehension

True or False

Write **T** or **F** for true or false.

_____ 1. Alberta works in a paper factory.

_____ 2. Alberta uses a special sewing machine.

_____ 3. Alberta sews linings into clothes.

_____ 4. Alberta works with about 10 other people.

_____ 5. Alberta says they all do different jobs.

_____ 6. Alberta says she has a good job.

Complete the Sentence

Read the story again. Fill in the blanks with the appropriate words from the story.

1. My _____ is Alberta.

2. I work in a _____ factory.

3. I use a special _____ machine.

4. I _____ linings into clothes.

5. I work with about 40 or 50 other _____.

6. We all do the _____ job.

7. I _____ this is a good job.

Language Skills

Structure Practice: Singular and Plural

Write the words for more than one.

    1. one hem   two   _____

    2. one seam   many _____

    3. one worker   four   _____

    4. one lining   five   _____

    5. one job   many _____

    6. one machine   ten   _____

Capital Letters: Names of People

Capital letters begin the names of people.

    Example: My name is **A**lberta **H**enderson.

Write the answer in the blank. Remember to use capital letters.

    1. What is your first name? _____

    2. What is your last name? _____

    3. What is your teacher's name? _____

    4. What is your best friend's name? _____

Structure Practice: Present Tense

Finish the paragraph using the words below.

makes   is   think   work   use   make

I _____ in a small bakery. The company

_____ bread and cakes. I _____ a mixer

to mix the dough. My work _____ a lot of fun.

I _____ our bread is very good. But I _____

better cakes at home.

Follow-up

Let's Talk about It
1. Where does Alberta work?
2. How many other people does she work with?
3. What does Alberta do at work?
4. Does Alberta like her job?
5. Why do you think she feels this way?

What's Your Story?
Do you have a good job? Why is it good? If you don't have a job, tell what you think would be a good job.

Do women in your country work?

5

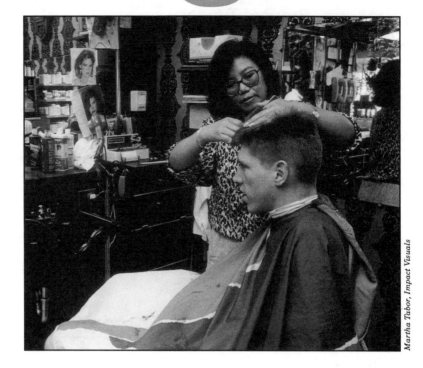

Martha Tabor, Impact Visuals

Women's Work

A lot of women in Puerto Rico work. They do many different jobs. They work in stores, in restaurants, in hospitals, in beauty shops, and in factories. They are waitresses, saleswomen, nurses, beauticians, and factory workers. They do the same jobs that women do in other parts of the United States. But they get less money and fewer benefits.

—Pilar Duyer
Puerto Rico

Comprehension

True or False

Write **T** or **F** for true or false.

_____ 1. A lot of women in Puerto Rico work.

_____ 2. They do the same jobs that women do in other parts of the
United States.

_____ 3. Women in Puerto Rico earn a lot more money than women in
other parts of the United States.

_____ 4. Some women work as waitresses.

_____ 5. Women in Puerto Rico do not work in factories.

Complete the Sentence

Read the story again. Fill in the blanks with the appropriate words from the
story.

1. A lot of _____ in Puerto Rico work.

2. They do many _____ jobs.

3. They work in stores, in _____ shops, in hospitals, and
in factories.

4. They are waitresses, nurses, and _____ workers.

5. They do the same _____ that women do in other parts
of the United States.

6. But they get less money and fewer _____.

Language Skills

Vocabulary Review

Match the job to its workplace.

Jobs	Workplaces
nurse	restaurant
waitress	store
beautician	hospital
saleswoman	beauty shop

Word Families

Circle the correct form.

1. The (beauty, beautician) cuts my hair.
2. My sister has a job as a (wait, waitress) in a restaurant.
3. Jane works in a (beauty, beautician) shop in the city.
4. Can you (wait, waiter) on us, please?
5. Sue is wearing a (beautician, beautiful) dress.

Structure Practice

Sometimes a few short sentences can be made into one long sentence. Read the short sentences:

1. They are nurses.
2. They are beauticians.
3. They are saleswomen.
4. They are waitresses.

Fill in the blanks in the long sentence with jobs from the short sentences.

They are _____, _____,

_____, and _____.

Read the short sentences. Then fill in the blanks in the long sentence with workplaces from the short sentences.

1. They work in restaurants.
2. They work in stores.
3. They work in hospitals.
4. They work in beauty shops.
5. They work in factories.

They work in _____, in _____, in

_____, in _____, and in

_____.

Follow-up

Let's Talk about It

1. Where do women in Puerto Rico work?
2. What kinds of jobs do they do?
3. Compare their jobs to women's jobs in other parts of the United States.
4. Who gets less money?
5. Who gets fewer benefits?
6. What other jobs do women do in the United States?

What's Your Story?

What kinds of jobs do women do in your country?

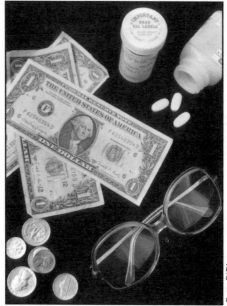

Patty DiRienzo

Money

At my job, the company pays me $4.25 per hour. It pays me by check. But the pay at this company never goes up. Everybody makes the same salary. My cousin has worked there for three years. She still gets the same pay.

And the benefits are no good. I get benefits only for prescription medicine and for glasses. I pay $80 a month for this health benefit. That is the rate for single people.

My salary is too low. I lose too much money to benefits and taxes. I hope I can leave this job soon.

—**Maria Velasquez**
Puerto Rico

Comprehension

True or False

Write **T** or **F** for true or false.

_____ 1. Maria's employer pays her by check.

_____ 2. The pay at Maria's company never goes up.

_____ 3. Maria likes the benefits at this job.

_____ 4. Maria wants to leave her job.

_____ 5. At Maria's company, single people pay $80 for health benefits.

_____ 6. Maria has worked at this company for three years.

Fill-in

Read the story again. Then write these words into the sentences.

taxes   rate   makes   benefits   pay   check

1. My company pays me by _____.

2. Everybody _____ the same salary.

3. The _____ are no good.

4. The _____ is too low.

5. I pay the _____ for single people.

6. I lose too much money to benefits and _____.

Language Skills

Vocabulary Review

Circle the correct word.

1. Maria needs a (prescription, company) to get her medicine.
2. We'll have to pay higher (taxes, glasses) to the state next year.
3. Soo Lim works for an insurance (company, salary).
4. She's going to the bank to deposit her (prescription, check).
5. Your pay is the same as your (salary, benefits).

Word Families

Circle the correct form.

1. I have to pick up my (prescribe, prescription) at the drugstore.
2. I get (medical, medicine) and dental benefits at my job.
3. Jane's doctor does not like to (prescribe, prescription) too much medicine.
4. If you take your (medical, medicine), you will feel better.
5. Do I need a (prescribe, prescription) for that?

Same Sound, Different Word

Read and study these groups of words:

there—their   too—to—two

Now circle the correct word for each sentence.

1. My salary is (too, to, two) low. I need more pay.
2. What time do you go (too, to, two) work?
3. Many children eat (there, their) lunch at school.
4. I have (too, to, two) sisters, Sonia and Carla.
5. I like New York, but I don't want to live (there, their).
6. I don't like July. It is always (too, to, two) hot!

Structure Practice: Verbs

Remember to add the -s ending to third person singular verbs.

Examples: The company pays Maria by check.

Everybody makes the same salary.

Now write the correct form of each verb into the story.

Maria _____ benefits only for prescription medicine and
(get)

for glasses. She _____ $80 a month for this health
(pay)

benefit. She _____ too much money to benefits and
(lose)

taxes. She _____ she can leave this job soon. If she
(hope)

_____ a better job, she will be happy.
(get)

Follow-up

Let's Talk about It

1. How much does Maria make per hour?
2. How does Maria get her salary?
3. What benefits does Maria get in this job?
4. How much do these benefits cost?
5. Why does Maria want to leave this job soon?
6. What will Maria want in her next job?

What's Your Story?

What benefits do workers usually get in your country?

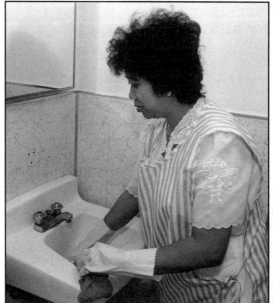

Is your job hard to do?

Rick Gerharter, Impact Visuals

A Hard Part of My Job

I'm a housekeeper. One of the most difficult activities of my job is cleaning room mirrors. Many times I have to stand on a chair to reach them. Sometimes I leave the mirrors uncleaned.

Sometimes I don't have enough time to finish this job. The family that I work for gives me too many rooms to clean each day. When the woman inspects the mirrors in all the rooms, she complains about my work.

For these reasons, cleaning room mirrors is the most difficult part of my job as a housekeeper.

—**Chantha Nou**
Cambodia

Comprehension

True or False

Write **T** or **F** for true or false.

_____ 1. Chantha works in a school.

_____ 2. It is easy for Chantha to clean room mirrors.

_____ 3. Chantha always cleans all of the mirrors.

_____ 4. The house has mirrors in more than one room.

Complete the Sentence

Read the story again. Fill in the blanks with the appropriate words from the story.

1. Chantha works as a _____.

2. One of her activities is cleaning room _____.

3. Sometimes she doesn't have enough _____.

4. The woman _____ the mirrors.

5. Sometimes the woman _____ about Chantha's work.

Language Skills

Vocabulary Review

Circle the correct word.

1. My boss (complains, inspects) when I am late.
2. Sometimes I don't have time to (reach, finish) my work.
3. She will inspect the room to see if it is (difficult, clean).
4. One (activity, housekeeper) of my job is sweeping floors.

Compound Words

Write the two words in each compound word. The first one is done for you.

sometimes	some	times
workday	_____	_____
housekeeper	_____	_____
storekeeper	_____	_____
saleswoman	_____	_____

Word Families

When you add the prefix **un-** to many words, it means "not."

Example: uncleaned = not cleaned

The mirrors are <u>not clean</u>.

Chantha leaves the mirrors <u>uncleaned</u>.

Choose the word that best completes the sentence and write it in the blank.

unopened   uncleaned   unpaid   undressed   unemployed

1. Chantha has to leave some rooms _____.

2. Your letter is still _____.

3. I get _____ before I go to bed.

4. When you don't have a job, you are _____ .

5. A housewife is an _____ worker.

Structure Practice

Read and study:

<u>this</u> job	<u>these</u> jobs
<u>this</u> woman	<u>these</u> women

Now write **this** or **these** to go with the words below.

1. _____ housekeeper   4. _____ rooms

2. _____ mirrors   5. _____ reasons

3. _____ chair   6. _____ mirror

Follow-up

Let's Talk about It

1. What is Chantha's job?
2. Why does she sometimes have to stand on a chair?
3. Why does Chantha's employer sometimes complain?
4. Why is it difficult for Chantha to clean room mirrors?
5. Do you think Chantha likes her job? Why or why not?

What's Your Story?

What is the most difficult activity in your job? Tell what you must do. Then say why it is difficult.

Amy Zuckerman, Impact Visuals

My Job

I work in a sample room. It is in a clothing factory. We make samples of children's clothes. Some of the workers cut the fabric. I sew the cut pieces together to make a complete garment. The factory managers decide if the factory will make these garments. The managers choose the styles that will sell the most in the big department stores.

My supervisor's name is Alma. She has a very good nature. I like to work with her. I am also very happy to work with the other people in my department. We work five days a week, eight hours a day.

We are always very busy. But I like to work because it is fun.

—**Priti Vyas**
India

Comprehension

True or False

Write **T** or **F** for true or false.

_____ 1. Priti works in a sample room.

_____ 2. She makes samples of women's clothes.

_____ 3. She sews pieces of fabric together.

_____ 4. Priti does not like her supervisor.

_____ 5. Priti says work is fun.

_____ 6. She works five days per week.

_____ 7. The workers choose the styles they will make.

Complete the Sentence

Read the story again. Fill in the blanks with the appropriate words from the story.

1. I work in a _____ room.

2. We make samples of children's _____.

3. Some of the workers cut the _____.

4. I sew the pieces of _____ together.

5. My _____ name is Alma.

6. I like the other people in my _____.

7. I like to work because it is _____.

Language Skills

Vocabulary Review

Circle the correct word.

1. I work in a (sample, factory) room.
2. I sew the (stores, pieces) together.
3. I make one complete (garment, department).
4. My supervisor has a good (nature, fabric).
5. I like to work because it is (fun, complete).
6. I work five days per (week, hour).
7. I work eight hours a (week, day).

Structure Practice

Use the words below to fill in the blanks. The first one is done for you.

1. supervisor   name

   What is your ___supervisor's___ ___name___ ?

2. children   toys

   There is a sale on _____ _____ at K-Mart.

3. manager   office

   The _____ _____ is on the top floor.

4. Yvonne   mother

   _____ _____ will help her get a job.

5. son   teacher

   My _____ _____ is a young man.

umber Work

underline the number word in each sentence. Then write the number for the
number word in the blank. The first one is done for you.

1. There are <u>eight</u> hours in an average work day. __8__

2. There are seven days in a week. _____

3. Many people start work at eight o'clock in the morning. _____

4. Many people finish working at five o'clock in the afternoon. _____

ow answer for yourself. Fill in with a number word.

1. I study _____ hours a day.

2. I watch TV _____ hours a day.

3. I work _____ hours a day.

4. I work _____ days a week.

'ollow-up

et's Talk about It

1. Where does Priti work?
2. Where is the sample room?
3. Who is Priti's supervisor?
4. What does Priti do?
5. How much time does she work?
6. Why does Priti like her supervisor?
7. Why does Priti like her job?

What's Your Story?

Do you think your job is fun? Tell about a job that you think would be fun.

_____

Kathleen Foster, Impact Visuals

How I Got My Job

My name is Yvonne. I came to the United States just a short time ago. I started working in America just a few months ago.

I really wanted to get a job, but I didn't know English. I asked my mother for help. She has worked in a factory for 10 or 12 years. She talked to her supervisors, and they said I could have a job.

Now I have a good job at the factory. I go to work with my mother every day. I'm glad she helped me get this job.

—Yvonne Largaespad
Nicaragu

omprehension

ue or False

rite **T** or **F** for true or false.

_____ 1. Yvonne works in a restaurant.

_____ 2. Yvonne didn't know English.

_____ 3. Yvonne talked to her mother.

_____ 4. Yvonne's mother worked in a factory for two years.

_____ 5. Yvonne really wanted to work.

_____ 6. Yvonne goes to work with her father.

_____ 7. Yvonne started working a few years ago.

omplete the Sentence

ead the story again. Fill in the blanks with the appropriate words from the ory.

1. My name is _____.

2. I came to _____ just a short time ago.

3. I started working in America just a few _____ ago.

4. I really wanted to _____, but I didn't know English.

5. I asked my _____ for help.

6. She has worked in a _____ for 10 or 12 years.

7. She talked to her _____, and they said I could have a job.

Language Skills

Structure Practice: Past Tense

Read the past tense verb form. Write the root word in the blank. The first one is done for you.

Past Tense	Root Word
1. started	_start_
2. wanted	_____
3. talked	_____
4. worked	_____
5. helped	_____
6. asked	_____

Now complete the story below by filling in the correct form of the verb in parentheses.

When I first came to America, my brother _____ me
(help)

get a job. I _____ him to help me, and he
(ask)

_____ to his supervisor. He told his supervisor that I
(talk)

_____ a job. I _____ that job
(want)   (start)

five years ago, and I still have it.

ructure Practice

ometimes two short sentences can be made into one long sentence.

Example: 1. His face is white.   2. He never smiles.

His face is white, and he never smiles.

1   2

ead the short sentences.

1. I really wanted to work.   2. I didn't know English.

ll in the blanks below to combine sentence 1 and sentence 2.

_____, but _____.

1   2

ead the short sentences.

3. My mother talked to her supervisors.   4. They gave me a job.

ll in the blanks below to combine sentence 3 and sentence 4.

_____, and _____.

3   4

ollow-up

et's Talk about It

1. Where is Yvonne from?
2. When did she start working in the United States?
3. What did Yvonne really want to do?
4. Why couldn't Yvonne get a job at first?
5. Who said Yvonne could have a job?
6. Who helped Yvonne get a job?

What's Your Story?

Do you have a job in the United States? How did you get your job? Did anyone help you?

10

Rick Gerharter, Impact Visuals

Respect

I started working in a restaurant when I was 18 years old. I worked 10 hours a day from Monday through Saturday. That was too many hours and too much hard work for me. Also, the pay wasn't good.

One day the owner of the restaurant started yelling at me. He criticized everything I did. He was very disrespectful. Then he told me that he wanted me to work more hours for the same pay. I told him he had to treat me with respect. Otherwise, I wouldn't stay.

—**Nilsa Rodrigue**
Puerto Ric

Comprehension

True or False

Write **T** or **F** for true or false.

_____ 1. Nilsa started working in a factory when she was 18 years old.

_____ 2. She worked eight hours a day.

_____ 3. She worked six days a week.

_____ 4. The pay was good.

_____ 5. The owner of the restaurant never criticized Nilsa.

_____ 6. The owner of the restaurant respected Nilsa.

Complete the Sentence

Read the story again. Fill in the blanks with the appropriate words from the story.

1. I started working in a _____ when I was 18 years old.

2. I worked 10 _____ a day from Monday through Saturday.

3. One day the _____ of the restaurant started yelling at me.

4. He _____ everything I did.

5. He was very _____.

6. I told him he had to treat me with _____.

Language Skills

Capital Letters: Days of the Week

Capital letters begin the names of the days of the week. Please rewrite the names of the days of the week correctly in the blanks. The first one is done for you.

sunday   __Sunday__

monday   _____

tuesday   _____

wednesday   _____

thursday   _____

friday   _____

saturday   _____

Same Sound, Different Word

Fill in the blanks in each sentence with **to**, **too**, or **two**.

1. I go _____ work every day.

2. She has _____ children.

3. They work _____ hard.

4. She works _____ many hours.

5. He has _____ jobs.

6. They go _____ work on weekends.

7. She told a story _____ the children.

Word Families

Circle the correct form.

1. The boss (critical, criticized) everything Nilsa did.
2. He was not (respect, respectful) of his workers.
3. Nilsa was treated with (disrespect, disrespectful).
4. Nilsa's boss was a (critical, criticize) person.
5. Teachers and students should (respect, respectful) each other.

Follow-up

Let's Talk about It

1. How old was Nilsa when she started working?
2. How long did she work each week?
3. How did the owner of the restaurant treat her?
4. What did the owner want Nilsa to do?
5. What did Nilsa tell the owner?
6. How do you think Nilsa felt?
7. What do you think happened after that?

What's Your Story?

Do you know a boss who is disrespectful of his/her workers? What do you do when someone shows you disrespect?

11

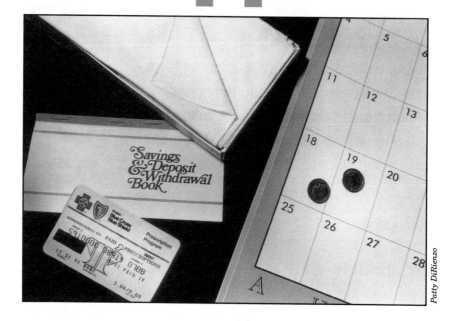

Patty DiRienzo

Take-home Pay

I work in a factory that makes handkerchiefs. My job is OK because I have friends there.

My job is not too difficult. I work at the machine that folds the handkerchiefs.

The salary is not so bad. Every month the company gives me 20¢ more. Now I get $4.70 per hour. I get paid every week, every Friday. I get paid by check.

The company deducts for social security, income tax, city tax—you know, everything! There is also Christmas Club. If you want to get Christmas Club, the company takes money out for that, too. It costs $10 every week.

I get Blue Cross in this job. It pays for the dentist, glasses, medicine, everything. For Blue Cross, I pay nothing.

—Margarita Vemba
Angola

omprehension

rite **T** or **F** for true or false.

_____ 1. Margarita works at Blue Cross.

_____ 2. Her salary goes up every month.

_____ 3. She gets paid by check.

_____ 4. She must pay for Blue Cross.

_____ 5. Blue Cross pays for her dentist bills.

_____ 6. Everyone where Margarita works gets Christmas Club.

anguage Skills

ocabulary Review

nish these sentences using the words below:

salary   income   check   social security   taxes   deduct

1. Most companies pay their employees by _____.

2. You can get _____ after you are 65 years old.

3. Our _____ pay for schools and roads.

4. Margarita's _____ is $4.70 per hour.

5. She pays tax based on her _____.

6. Most companies _____ money for social security.

Structure Practice

Finish the sentences below using the words at the right with the word **per**.

Example: Now I get ___$4.70 per hour___. ($4.70/hour)

1. The tickets cost _____. ($10.00/person)

2. My company gives me _____ for vacation.
(two weeks/year)

3. My doctor says to take this medicine _____.
(three times/day)

4. The dinner costs _____. ($10.95/person)

5. This hotel charges _____ for a single room.
($49.00/night)

6. The speed limit here is _____. (55 miles/hou

Capital Letters: Holidays

Use capital letters when you write the names of holidays.

Example: Christmas

Rewrite the names of the holidays below with capital letters.

1. thanksgiving   _____

2. president's day   _____

3. independence day   _____

4. new year's eve   _____

5. halloween   _____

6. labor day   _____

umber Work

ead and study:

20 cents $.20   20¢

ow write. The first one is done for you.

1.	25 cents	$.25	25¢
2.	_____	$.75	_____
3.	_____	_____	12¢
4.	52 cents	_____	_____
5.	_____	$.02	_____

Follow-up

et's Talk about It

1. Why is Margarita's job OK?
2. What is her job at the factory?
3. How much does she get paid for one hour's work?
4. When does she get paid?
5. Does everyone get Christmas Club at Margarita's company?
6. How much does Blue Cross cost at Margarita's company?

What's Your Story?

What benefits do you get in your job?

12

Patty DiRienzo

Where I Work

I work in the parking lot at the airport. I am a cashier there.

The airport is far from my house. It takes me 30 minutes to drive to work. But with no car it takes me one hour. First I must take the subway. Then I get a bus.

At the airport you can see one very big building. That is the terminal. The parking lot is near the terminal. It has 10 tollbooths. Usually, there is a cashier in each tollbooth. The cashiers collect money from people who are leaving the parking lot.

All the tollbooths are under one long roof. Five lanes enter the tollbooth building from the street. Five lanes exit to the street. There are always a lot of cars in the parking lot.

—Marie Cange
Haiti

Comprehension

True or False

Write **T** or **F** for true or false.

_____ 1. Marie works in the airport terminal.

_____ 2. The terminal at Marie's airport is a very big building.

_____ 3. There are 10 parking lots at the airport where Marie works.

_____ 4. All the tollbooths are under one roof.

_____ 5. Marie sometimes drives to work.

_____ 6. Usually, there is a cashier in every tollbooth.

_____ 7. The airport is near Marie's house.

Fill-in

Read the story again. Then write these words into the sentences.

First   there   always   Usually   But

1. I work in the parking lot. I am a cashier _____.

2. It takes me 30 minutes to drive to work. _____ with no car it takes me one hour.

3. _____ I take the subway. Then I get a bus.

4. The airport has 10 tollbooths. _____, there is a cashier in each one.

5. There are _____ a lot of cars in the parking lot.

Language Skills

Vocabulary Review

Write the words below into the story.

parking lot   terminal   airport   tollbooth   cashier

Today I am going to take an airplane to visit my family. First, I will drive

to the _____. I will leave my car in the _____.

Then I will go to the _____. From this building, I will get

on the airplane.

When I come home again, I will find my car and drive to the exit. I will

stop at the _____ to pay for parking. I will give my money

to the _____, and then I will drive home.

Structure Practice: Prepositions

Choose the word that best completes each sentence and write it in the
blank. You may use a word more than once.

in   near   at   under   from

1. Marie works _____ a parking lot.

2. The parking lot is _____ the airport.

3. The parking lot is _____ the terminal.

4. All the tollbooths are _____ one roof.

5. The cars enter the tollbooths _____ the street.

6. There is usually a cashier _____ each tollbooth.

Structure Practice

"It takes me" + a time expression answers the question "How long?"

Example: How long does it take you to drive to work?

It takes me 30 minutes to drive to work.

Complete the sentences. Write answers about yourself.

1. It takes me _____ to prepare dinner.

2. It takes me _____ to get to work.

3. It takes me _____ to clean my home.

4. It takes me five minutes to _____.

5. It takes me 30 minutes to _____.

6. _____ to get to my English class.

Follow-up

Let's Talk about It

1. Where does Marie work?
2. What is her job?
3. How does Marie go to work?
4. How many tollbooths are there?
5. What does a cashier do?
6. What are airports like in your country?

What's Your Story?

How do you get to work? How do you get to class? How long does it take you?

13

THE BETTMAN ARCHIVE

New on the Job

I work in a belt factory. This is my first job in America. The job is hard because nobody knows me. I can't speak English. Nobody helps me, just my cousin. My cousin works at the same factory. She is my friend. She works near me. My cousin helps me do the job. I must learn everything.

In this job I'm like a child. I can't speak. I don't understand what people say to me. I never know if they want me to do something. I'm nervous all day.

I will work in this place for about one month. Then I will work in another place. My cousin knows about a hotel downtown. The hotel always needs cleaning ladies. That will be a better job.

—**Maria Velasquez**
Puerto Rico

Comprehension

True or False

Write **T** or **F** for true or false.

_____ 1. Maria works in a hotel.

_____ 2. Maria's sister works in the same place.

_____ 3. For this job, Maria must learn everything.

_____ 4. Maria speaks English well.

_____ 5. Maria is nervous about her job.

_____ 6. Maria wants to leave this job.

Fill-in

Read the story again. Write these words into the sentences.

first	hotel	cousin	nervous
hard	child	understand	

1. This is my _____ job in America.

2. The job is _____.

3. Nobody helps me, just my _____.

4. In this job I'm like a _____.

5. I don't _____ what people say to me.

6. I'm _____ all day.

7. A _____ downtown needs cleaning ladies.

Language Skills

Compound Words

Put together the first and second parts of the compound words below.

no   body   _____

some   thing   _____

down   town   _____

every   thing   _____

Now form three other compound words from the words in the first two columns above.

_____

_____

_____

Structure Practice: Singular and Plural

Read and study the difference for one and more than one:

one factory   two factories
one lady   three ladies

Now write the plural for these words.

1. one country   many _____

2. one salary   two _____

3. one city   five _____

4. one baby   some _____

Structure Practice: Verbs

Circle the correct form of the verb in each sentence. All the sentences are in the story.

1. I (work, works) in a factory.
2. I don't understand what people (say, says) to me.
3. My cousin (work, works) at the same factory.
4. She (help, helps) me with my job.
5. I never (know, knows) what people want.
6. My cousin (know, knows) about a hotel downtown.
7. The hotel always (need, needs) cleaning ladies.

Follow-up

Let's Talk about It

1. Where does Maria work?
2. Why is her job hard?
3. Who works at the same factory?
4. Why is Maria like a child in this job?
5. How long will she work in this place?
6. What will be the next place where she works?
7. What will be her job there?

What's Your Story?

What was your first job in America? How did you learn your job?

14

Harvey Finkle, Impact Visuals

The Boss and the Supervisor

I work in a pill packing plant. I like my job. My boss is friendly and helpful. He is our line leader. Each group of workers has one line leader. Our line packs the pills to mail. The line leader stands at the end of the line. He makes sure our work is good. He is the last person who looks at the pill boxes.

My supervisor doesn't do much with the employees. Sometimes he comes into the packing room. He looks at how we do the job. He always leaves very quickly.

Most of the time he works with money. He writes down all the company's expenses. He also writes down how much money the plant makes. He keeps these accounts in a large red book.

All day long he sits in a little room. His face is white, and he never smiles. I like my job better.

—**Valentina Riva**
Nicaragua

Comprehension

True or False

Write **T** or **F** for true or false.

_____ 1. Valentina is an employee at a pill packing plant.

_____ 2. Valentina is a line leader.

_____ 3. Valentina is the last person who looks at the pill boxes.

_____ 4. The supervisor leaves the packing room very quickly.

_____ 5. The supervisor keeps the accounts in a large red book.

_____ 6. Most of the time, the line leader works with money.

Who's in the story?

Based on the story, answer **employee**, **boss**, or **supervisor** for these questions.

1. Who stands at the end of the pill packing line?_____

2. Who packs the pills to mail?_____

3. Who makes sure the work is good?_____

4. Who works with money?_____

5. Who writes down the company's expenses?_____

6. Who looks at the pill boxes last?_____

7. Who works in a little room?_____

8. Who is Valentina?_____

Language Skills

Structure Practice: Prepositions

Choose the word that best completes each sentence and write it in the blank. All the phrases are in the story. You may use a word more than once.

   in   of   at   into   with

1. I work _____ a plant.

2. My boss stands _____ the end of our line.

3. Each group _____ workers has a line leader.

4. Sometimes, my supervisor comes _____ the packing room.

5. Most of the time, he works _____ money.

6. He sits _____ a little room.

7. He keeps the accounts _____ a large red book.

Structure Practice: Verbs

Circle the correct form of the verb in each sentence. All the sentences are from the story.

1. I (work, works) in a pill packing plant.
2. I (like, likes) my job in the plant.
3. Our line (pack, packs) the pills to mail.
4. The line leader (make, makes) sure our work is good.
5. He (look, looks) at the pill boxes.
6. Sometimes my supervisor (come, comes) into the room.
7. He (sit, sits) in a little room and (count, counts) the money.
8. I (like, likes) my job better.

Structure Practice: Adjectives

Adjectives tell us more about people, places, and things. When we use adjectives, we can put them after the word we describe.

Example: My job is <u>hard</u>.

We can also put adjectives before the word we describe.

Example: I have a <u>hard</u> job.

Now look at these sentences from the story. Write each sentence again with the adjective before the word it describes. The first one is done for you.

1. My boss is friendly. I have a _____<u>friendly boss</u>_____.

2. Our work must be good. We must do _____.

3. His book is large. He has a _____.

4. His face is white. He has a _____.

5. His room is little. He sits in a _____.

Follow-up

Let's Talk about It

1. What kind of work does Valentina do?
2. What kind of job does Valentina's boss have?
3. What kind of person is he?
4. What does her supervisor do?
5. How much time does he spend with the employees?
6. What kind of person is he?
7. In your opinion, why does Valentina like her job?

What's Your Story?

Whose job would you rather have, yours or your supervisor's? Why?

15

Help from My Friends

My first job in America is the job I have now. It is at Ashbourne Country Club. I started a year ago. First I was a pot washer. Then I got a promotion. Now I help decorate party rooms.

It wasn't difficult to find this job. I talked to my friends, and they helped me.

"Ashbourne Country Club needs employees," they said. "You can speak English or not speak English. It doesn't matter. Go, Sergio. Maybe you will get a job."

So, one day I went to this club and filled out the application. One week later, I started work.

I was in America for just two months when I got this job. With friends it was easy.

—**Sergio Cabrera**
Argentina

Comprehension

True or False
Write **T** or **F** for true or false.

_____ 1. Sergio is working in the kitchen at Ashbourne Country Club.

_____ 2. Sergio's friends helped him find his first job in America.

_____ 3. Sergio had to speak English to get a job.

_____ 4. Sergio started to work one month after he applied for the job.

_____ 5. It was hard for Sergio to get a job.

_____ 6. Sergio still works at Ashbourne Country Club.

Fill-in
Read the story again. Then write these words into the sentences:

promotion   decorate   difficult   friends

application   employees

1. Sergio's _____ helped him get a job.

2. Because Sergio did well, his boss gave him a _____
   and more pay.

3. The country club needed more _____.

4. To get his job, Sergio had to fill out an _____.

5. Sergio's job is to _____ party rooms.

6. Sergio said that it was not _____ to get this job.

Language Skills

Word Families

Circle the correct form.

1. I am here to (apply, application) for a job.
2. Sergio got a (promoted, promotion) after a few months.
3. You must fill out a job (application, promotion).
4. Sergio was (promoted, applied) to a better job.
5. I (applied, application) for the job, but I didn't get it.

Word Families

For many jobs, we add an **-er** to a verb to make a name for the person who does the job. If the verb ends in **e**, we add only an **-r**.

Examples: If you wash pots, you are a pot <u>washer</u>.

                           If you bake cakes, you are a <u>baker</u>.

Write the name for the person who does the job that is underlined in each sentence.

1. If you <u>teach</u> school, you are a _____.

2. If you <u>paint</u> houses, you are a _____.

3. If you <u>work</u> in a factory, you are a factory _____.

4. If you <u>write</u> books, you are a _____.

5. If you <u>sing</u> for a living, you are a _____.

6. If you <u>drive</u> trucks, you are a truck _____.

7. If you <u>report</u> the news, you are a _____.

apital Letters: Names of Places

When the words for a place are its name, all the words in the name begin with capital letters. Offices and businesses are places that can have names. Places in a city can have names, too:

Examples: Ashbourne Country Club   Market Street

Write these names for locations. Use capital letters.

1. chestnut street   _____

2. fenway park   _____

3. acme trucking company   _____

4. fisher's restaurant   _____

5. golden gate bridge   _____

Follow-up

Let's Talk about It

1. What was Sergio's first job in America?
2. After his promotion, what was his job?
3. Where does he work now?
4. Who helped him to find this job?
5. How long was he in America when he got this job?
6. Why was it easy for Sergio to get this job?

What's Your Story?

How did you get your first job in America? What did you have to do? Was it easy or difficult?